W9-BYP-677

POPE BENEDICT XVI

St. Paul

Spiritual Thoughts Series

Preface by Cardinal Tarcisio Bertone
Introduction by Edmund Caruana, O.Carm.

United States Conference of Catholic Bishops
Washington, D.C.

Cover photo: *L'Osservatore Romano*

First printing, August 2008

ISBN: 978-1-60137-053-2

CONTENTS

t. Paul cries to us in God's Name: "Your attitude must be Christ's—*Touto phroneite en hymin ho kai en Christo Iesou*." Learn to think as Christ thought, learn to think with him! And this thinking is not only the thinking of the mind, but also a thinking of the heart.

Pope Benedict XVI
Homily, November 7, 2006

PREFACE

he figure of Paul, on whom we focus our thoughts during the celebration of the Year of St. Paul by recalling the bimillennium of the Apostle's birth, profoundly challenges us even today. His journey on the road to Damascus in itself signifies a true spiritual journey that, in a certain sense, reproduces the experience of all who are set free from the illusions and fantasies that influence them and who achieve their own authenticity. The term Paul uses to describe this decisive experience is "vocation." Paul knew that his conversion was not the result of an evolution in his thinking or reflections, but rather the fruit of an unforeseeable divine grace. It is necessary, first, to attribute to God this initial movement that sets us free from all sterile activism and places us in his love, his *caritas*, assigning us a gratuitous place where we can cultivate our vocation and our faith.

But the road to Damascus is also, second, a place of meeting, of an encounter with Jesus, of Jesus who approaches those who until that moment did not know or recognize him, as has so often happened in our own personal stories. The same thing also happened to those travelers to Emmaus. The circumstances are always the same. It is always Jesus who comes to meet those who are preoccupied or incredulous, if not actually hostile, as was the case with Paul. And after this encounter with grace, their lives are bound to be transformed by it. Paul's life demonstrates this. It is an ongoing witness to this encounter and to what flows from it: the resulting need to refer to it always, to center our lives on Jesus, to learn from him, to adopt his attitudes in order to realize ourselves fully.

The third stage, which in a certain sense completed Paul's spiritual journey, was that of mission. His task would be to carry the Lord's name "before Gentiles, kings and Israelites" (Acts 9:15), to carry Christ. Those who have met Christ and come into contact with him cannot keep him for themselves. Think of Mary's joyful journey to Elizabeth after the divine conception. The task upon returning to Damascus is one of mission: to share, to communicate the experience of love, of God's grace and Christ's joy, that has been revealed to us and come to us on the world's roads, which are not always smooth and easy. But the announcement of mission contains in itself another revelation as well, that of the Cross: "I will show him," says the Lord, "what he will have to suffer for my name" (Acts 9:16). The Cross tells us that our way of self-giving must be that of Jesus, who gave himself to us by renouncing every privilege, emptying himself, choosing to serve. This is the cross that St. Paul also carried in his life, which was filled with passion for Jesus but also with much pain and suffering, and which ended in the shedding of his blood. I hope that the thoughts contained in this book may accompany readers on a similar spiritual journey, and that from their encounter with Jesus their lives may be genuinely transformed, as was the life of Paul and of all who in every age believe and trust in him.

✠ Cardinal Tarcisio Bertone
Secretary of State of His Holiness

Introduction

hen Pope Benedict XVI announced a jubilee year from June 28, 2008, to June 29, 2009, to commemorate the bimillennium of the birth of the Apostle Paul, among the activities for promoting a fresh approach to Pauline spirituality he mentioned "liturgical, cultural and ecumenical events" and "pastoral and social initiatives." Along with study conventions, he expressed hope for "special publications on Pauline texts . . . in order to make ever more widely known the immense wealth of the teaching they contain" (Homily, June 28, 2007).

The present volume is situated in the context of this direction proposed by the Holy Father. Its aim is to provide a reading of St. Paul from the special perspective of a collection of the Pope's thoughts and reflections that refer specifically to this extraordinary witness of faith in a humanity redeemed by Christ.

Pope Benedict interprets St. Paul's spiritual trajectory by starting with a very simple question: "How does a human being's encounter with Christ occur?" (Audience, November 8, 2006). The answer he gives serves to make more explicit the outlines of belief in Christ, not only for Paul but for every Christian. Reflecting on Paul's conversion, Benedict XVI emphasizes that it did not result from a reasoning process or from merely human logic, but from a divine intervention, "an unforeseeable, divine grace" (Audience, October 25, 2006). The Pope emphasizes that the case of Paul places us at once face to face with "this restraint from seeking oneself by oneself but instead receiving oneself from Christ" (Audience, November 8, 2006), which is the first characteristic of Christian identity. "Before his conversion, Paul had not been a man distant from God and from his Law. On the contrary, he had been observant, with an observance faithful to the point of fanaticism" (Audience, November 8, 2006). But in the light of his encounter with Christ, Paul understood that he had been seeking to build up himself and his own justice.

Paul's experience on the road to Damascus invites us to recognize God's action in our lives and to become ever more aware of this movement from God to us, which represents the most universal element of our faith. "Indeed, it is to him and his grace alone," comments Pope Benedict, "that we owe what we are as Christians" (Audience, November 8, 2006). The kind of anthropological reflection that has made a similar "discovery" about humans today—used to trusting exclusively in their own strength and regarding themselves as the sole creator of their destinies—is evident. *Homo faber* ("man the maker") is unable to admit that not everything depends on human beings, that not everything can be expressed and encompassed in a human project. To this modern *homo faber*, Paul teaches that we can see and understand only if God allows us, and that we find ourselves only when we are found. To say that God is grace means that not everything depends on us: that the action, the first movement is made by him. It is God who calls, God who chooses, God who works. It is he who first loved us, writes John the evangelist (1 Jn 4:19). We can only enter into this movement and second it, trying to understand it ever more deeply in order to follow more closely his call and his will.

But Paul's life, starting with his call on the road to Damascus, also bears witness to another decision and resolution: to make Christ the center of his life. Pope Benedict says that "giving oneself with Christ, thereby participating personally in the life of Christ himself," is the other basic element of Christian identity that Paul constantly manifested by his preaching and by his whole life (Audience, November 8, 2006). To place Christ at the center of our life means to act in such a way that our life is marked "by the encounter, by communion with Christ and with his word" (Audience, October 25, 2006). For Paul "it was not enough to say that Christians are baptized or believers; for him, it was just as important to say they are 'in Christ Jesus'" (Audience, November 8, 2006). Pope Benedict notes that this mutual compenetration between Christ and the Christian, which St. Paul summarizes in the expression "Christ is in you" (Rom 8:10; 2 Cor 13:5, etc.), has an almost mystical connotation. Just as Christ became human, we too must become incarnate in Christ and enter into his sentiments of "compassion, kindness, humility, gentleness, and patience" (Col 3:12), becoming his disciples in our willingness to bear and forgive, and his imitators in our ability to love.

Pope Benedict constantly invites us to imitate Paul, drawing on the exhortation left by the Apostle to be imitators of him, as he was of Christ (cf. Audience, October 25, 2006). The incarnate Word has the power to transform human existence from within and, by the life-giving activity of his Spirit, to raise human beings to the dignity of children of God (cf. Rom 8:14-17). "This is our greatest dignity," explains the Pope, "to be not merely images but also children of God" (Audience, November 15, 2006). The presence of the Spirit of the Lord in our hearts is a guarantee and assurance of this divine sonship that distinguishes us from slaves "who are not free to do otherwise." It gives us the freedom of sons and daughters, or the freedom of one who, being the heir (cf. Rom 8:17), feels responsible for the inheritance entrusted by the father. In the face of false freedoms, which often coexist with arbitrary acts and end in self-annihilation, Pope Benedict, reading this passage from St. Paul, draws an important lesson for today and teaches us that freedom and responsibility go together: "true freedom is demonstrated in responsibility, in a way of behaving in which one takes upon oneself a shared responsibility for the world, for oneself and for others" (Homily, June 3, 2006).

The centrality of Christ; our adoption as children thanks to the Spirit; the spiritual reality of the Church as depository of the mystery of Christ—the body of Christ according to St. Paul's definition; meditations on Baptism and the Eucharist that reflect deeply the Christian's communion with Christ and being in Christ; the priest as one who brings God to men and women (Speech, December 22, 2006); the life of prayer in which we search for God's will (Homily, January 25, 2008); the pursuit of holiness as a realization of "what we already are, raised to the dignity of God's adopted children, in Christ Jesus" (Angelus, November 1, 2005)—these are just a few of the topics among the many treated by Pope Benedict in this great catechesis on St. Paul. As our collection of these thoughts shows, the Holy Father has been developing this catechesis since the beginning of his pontificate, and he has regarded it as a priority of his teaching office. It is no accident that, immediately after his election as Pope, he decided to visit the Basilica of St. Paul Outside-the-Walls and place all his activities as pastor of the universal Church under the patronage of the tireless Apostle of Christ. On that occasion, drawing his inspiration from St. Paul, he emphasized his decision "to [make] Christ the center of his life, leaving all things for the sublimity of knowing him and the mystery of his love, and subsequently, striving to proclaim him to all, especially the pagans, 'that we may spread his name' (Rom 1:5)" (Homily, April 25, 2005). With these words of his from that time we want to close this brief presentation. Indeed, in one short sentence they manage to condense Paul's essential lesson "to set out anew from Christ" and "to prefer nothing to the love of Christ" (St. Benedict, Rule 4: *Nihil amori Christi praeponere*), which is the leitmotif of all Pope Benedict's pontificate, and at the same time the only true rule of life for Christians of all times.

Edmund Caruana, O.Carm.
Managing Editor,
Libreria Editrice Vaticana

St. Paul

The love of Christ impels us. (2 Cor 5:14)

1. *The beginning*

I give thanks to God who, at the beginning of my ministry as Successor of Peter, has granted me to pause in prayer at the Apostle Paul's tomb. It is a deeply-desired pilgrimage, an act of faith that I am making not only in my own name but also in the name of the beloved Diocese of Rome, of which the Lord has constituted me Bishop and Pastor, and of the universal Church, entrusted to my pastoral care. It is a pilgrimage, so to speak, to the roots of mission, the mission that the Risen Christ entrusted to Peter, to the Apostles and in a special way also to Paul, urging him to proclaim the Gospel to the Gentiles, so that he came as far as this city where, after preaching the Kingdom of God for some time (cf. Acts 28:31), he poured out his blood, bearing the extreme witness to his Lord who had "grasped" him (Phil 3:12) and sent him forth.

Homily at the Basilica of St. Paul Outside-the-Walls
April 25, 2005

I. THE APOSTOLIC VOCATION

1. Apostle to the Gentiles

2. On the road to Damascus

In fact, the Lord's call to Paul on the road to Damascus brought him to this: to making Christ the center of his life, leaving all things for the sublimity of knowing him and the mystery of his love, and subsequently, striving to proclaim him to all, especially the pagans, "that we may spread his name" (Rom 1:5).

> *Homily at the Basilica of St. Paul Outside-the-Walls*
> *April 25, 2005*

3. Bringing Christ

On the road to Damascus, Christ's radiant face and strong voice had snatched him from his violent zeal as a persecutor and had kindled within him the new zeal of the Crucified One, who reconciles in his Cross those who are near and far (cf. Eph 2:11-22). Paul realized that in Christ the whole of the law is fulfilled and that those who adhere to Christ are united with him and fulfill the law. Bringing Christ, and with Christ the one God, to all peoples became his mission.

> *Homily in Assisi on the eighth centenary*
> *of the conversion of St. Francis*
> *June 17, 2007*

4. *Proclaiming the Gospel*

St. Paul traveled tirelessly, taking the Gospel with him. He even felt under a sort of "compulsion" to proclaim the Gospel (cf. 1 Cor 9:16)—not so much out of concern for the salvation of the single non-baptized person who had not yet been reached by the Gospel, but rather because he was aware that history as a whole could not attain fulfillment until the Gospel had reached the full number (*pléroma*) of Gentiles (cf. Rom 11:25).

> *Christmas greeting to the Roman Curia*
> *December 21, 2007*

5. *The God of all people*

Another fundamental lesson offered by Paul is the universal breadth that characterizes his apostolate. Acutely feeling the problem of the Gentiles, of the pagans, to know God, who in Jesus Christ Crucified and Risen offers salvation to all without exception, he dedicates himself to make this Gospel—literally, "good news"—known, to announce the grace destined to reconcile men with God, self and others. From the first moment he understood that this is a reality that did not concern only the Jews or a certain group of men, but one that had a universal value and concerned everyone, because God is the God of everyone.

General Audience
October 25, 2006

6. *Paul's preaching*

After his encounter with the Risen Christ on the road to Damascus, . . . [Paul] took up the Christological interpretation of the Old Testament . . . deepening and completing it, and consequently became the "Apostle to the Gentiles." The Law is fulfilled, he taught, in the Cross of Christ. And faith in Christ, communion with Christ's love, is the true fulfillment of all the Law. This is the content of Paul's preaching. He showed in this way that the God of Abraham had become the God of all. And all believers in Jesus Christ, as children of Abraham, shared in the promises.

General Audience
January 10, 2007

7. *Catholicity*

Strangers have become friends; crossing every border, we recognize one another as brothers and sisters. This brings to fulfillment the mission of St. Paul, who knew that he was the "minister of Christ Jesus among the Gentiles, with the priestly duty of preaching the Gospel of God so that the Gentiles [might] be offered up as a pleasing sacrifice, consecrated by the Holy Spirit" (Rom 15:16). The purpose of the mission is that humanity itself becomes a living glorification of God, the true worship that God expects: this is the deepest meaning of *catholicity*—a *catholicity* that has already been given to us, towards which we must constantly start out again.

Homily on the Solemnity of SS. Peter and Paul
June 29, 2005

8. *Faced with death*

"I for my part am already being poured out like a libation," he writes to the Apostle Timothy. "The time of my dissolution is near. I have fought the good fight, I have finished the race, I have kept the faith" (2 Tm 4:6-7). Paul, in prison in Rome, saw death approaching and sketched an evaluation full of recognition and hope. He was at peace with God and with himself and faced death serenely, in the knowledge that he had spent his whole life, sparing no effort, at the service of the Gospel.

Angelus
October 28, 2007

9. *Paul's example*

As in early times, today too Christ needs apostles ready to sacrifice themselves. He needs witnesses and martyrs like St. Paul. Paul, a former violent persecutor of Christians, when he fell to the ground dazzled by the divine light on the road to Damascus, did not hesitate to change sides to the Crucified One and followed him without second thoughts. He lived and worked for Christ, for him he suffered and died. How timely his example is today!

Homily at First Vespers, Solemnity of SS. Peter and Paul
June 28, 2007

2. By Grace

10. *The choice of believers*

In the beginning [says St. Paul], "before the creation of the world" (Eph 1:4), in the eternity of God, divine grace is available to act. I am moved in meditating on this truth: from all eternity we are present in the eyes of God, and he has decided to save us.

I Salmi dei Vespri (The Psalms of Vespers)
(Vatican City: Libreria Editrice Vaticana, 2006)

11. *The call*

[Paul] will explicitly define himself as "apostle by vocation" (cf. Rom 1:1; 1 Cor 1:1) or "apostle by the will of God" (2 Cor 1:1; Eph 1:1; Col 1:1), as if to emphasize that his conversion was not the result of a development of thought or reflection, but the fruit of divine intervention, an unforeseeable, divine grace.

General Audience
October 25, 2006

12. *By grace*

Divine charity is the strength that transforms the life of Saul of Tarsus and makes him the Apostle to the Gentiles. Writing to the Christians at Corinth, St. Paul confesses that God's grace worked the extraordinary event of conversion in him: "By the grace of God I am what I am, and his grace toward me was not in vain" (1 Cor 15:10). On the one hand, he feels the weight of having hindered the spread of Christ's message; but on the other, he lives in the joy of having met the Risen Lord and having been enlightened and transformed by his light.

Homily at the Basilica of St. Paul Outside-the-Walls
January 25, 2006

13. *The power of grace*

"I worked harder than any of them, though it was not I, but the grace of God which is with me" (1 Cor 15:10). Tirelessly, as though the work of the mission depended entirely upon his own efforts, St. Paul was nevertheless always motivated by the profound conviction that all his energy came from God's grace at work in him.

Homily at the Basilica of St. Paul Outside-the-Walls
January 25, 2008

14. *Apostle by vocation*

Paul knew he was "called to be an apostle," that is, that he had not presented himself as a candidate, nor was his a human appointment, but solely by a divine call and election. The Apostle to the Gentiles repeats several times in his Letters that his whole life is a fruit of God's freely given and merciful grace (cf. 1 Cor 15:9-10; 2 Cor 4:1; Gal 1:15). He was chosen to proclaim "the Gospel of God" (Rom 1:1), to disseminate the announcement of divine Grace which in Christ reconciles man with God, himself and others.

Homily at First Vespers, Solemnity of SS. Peter and Paul
June 28, 2007

15. *The grace of Christ*

[In Ephesus] the Apostle wishes them "grace and peace from God our Father and the Lord Jesus Christ" (Eph 1:2). *Grace* is the power that transforms man and the world; *peace* is the mature fruit of this transformation. Christ is grace; Christ is peace.

Homily in Ephesus during his apostolic journey to Turkey
November 29, 2006

II. The Encounter with Jesus

3. Christ, the Face of God

16. *The greatness of the Revelation*

God did not only speak, but loved us very realistically; he loved us to the point of the death of his own Son. It is precisely here that we are shown the full grandeur of revelation that has, as it were, inflicted the wounds in the heart of God himself. Then each one of us can say personally, together with St. Paul, I live "a life of faith in the Son of God, who loved me and gave himself for me" (Gal 2:20). Let us pray to the Lord that the truth of these words may be deeply impressed in our hearts, together with his joy and with his responsibility.

Homily on the Solemnity of SS. Peter and Paul
June 29, 2005

17. *To know God*

The subject "God" is essential. St. Paul says in his Letter to the Ephesians: "Remember that you were at that time . . . having no hope and without God. . . . But now in Christ Jesus you who once were far off have been brought near" (Eph 2:12-13). Thus, life has a meaning that guides me even through difficulties. It is therefore necessary to return to God the Creator, to the God who is creative reason, and then to find Christ, who is the living Face of God.

Lenten meeting with the clergy of Rome
February 22, 2007

18. *Profession of faith*

St. Paul also says in another passage of his First Letter to the Corinthians: "Although there may be so-called gods in heaven or on earth" . . . for us there is only "one God, the Father, from whom are all things and for whom we exist, and one Lord, Jesus Christ, through whom are all things and through whom we exist" (1 Cor 8:5-6). Thus, from the outset the disciples recognized the Risen Jesus as the One who is our brother in humanity but is also one with God; the One who, with his coming into the world and throughout his life, in his death and in his Resurrection, brought us God and in a new and unique way made God present in the world: the One, therefore, who gives meaning and hope to our life; in fact, it is in him that we encounter the true Face of God that we find what we really need in order to live.

*Address to the participants in the
convention of the Diocese of Rome
June 11, 2007*

19. *Hope*

"May he [God the Father] enlighten your innermost vision that you may know the great hope to which he has called you, the wealth of his glorious heritage" in the saints (Eph 1:18). This is the hope that St. Paul raises to the God of Our Lord Jesus Christ, the Father of glory. . . . We can never thank God, Our Father, enough for this immense treasure of hope and glory that he has given to us in his Son Jesus. Our constant commitment is to let ourselves be continuously enlightened by him, so as to become more and more deeply acquainted with his mysterious gift.

Presentation of the Compendium of the
Catechism of the Catholic Church
May 28, 2005

4. The Centrality of Christ

20. *A lesson*

[Paul's] existence would become that of an Apostle who wants to "become all things to all men" (1 Cor 9:22) without reserve. From here we draw a very important lesson: what counts is to place Jesus Christ at the center of our lives, so that our identity is marked essentially by the encounter, by communion with Christ and with his Word.

General Audience
October 25, 2006

21. *The project*

The Apostle to the Gentiles has just reminded us that if we die with Christ, "we shall also live with him; if we endure, we shall also reign with him; if we deny him, he also will deny us" (2 Tm 2:11-12). The entire plan of life of the Christian can only be modeled on Christ, all of it with him, for him and in him, to the glory of God the Father.

Homily at the funeral Mass of
Cardinal Alfonso Maria Stickler
December 14, 2007

22. *Self-giving*

"The life I now live in the flesh I live by faith in the Son of God, who loved me and gave himself for me" (Gal 2:20). Paul, therefore, no longer lives for himself, for his own justice. He lives for Christ and with Christ: in giving of himself, he is no longer seeking and building himself up. This is the new justice, the new orientation given to us by the Lord, given to us by faith. Before the Cross of Christ, the extreme expression of his self-giving, there is no one who can boast of himself, of his own self-made justice, made for himself!

General Audience
November 8, 2006

23. *Christian identity*

[The] Christian identity is composed of precisely two elements: this restraint from seeking oneself by oneself but instead receiving oneself from Christ and giving oneself with Christ, thereby participating personally in the life of Christ himself to the point of identifying with him and sharing both his death and his life. This is what Paul wrote in his *Letter to the Romans*: "All of us . . . were baptized into his death . . . we were buried therefore with him . . . we have been united with him. . . . So you also must consider yourselves dead to sin and alive to God in Christ Jesus" (Rom 6:3, 4, 5, 11).

General Audience
November 8, 2006

24. *Mystical union*

Although faith unites us closely to Christ, it emphasizes the distinction between us and him; but according to Paul, Christian life also has an element that we might describe as "mystical," since it entails an identification of ourselves with Christ and of Christ with us.

General Audience
November 8, 2006

25. *Conquered*

Peter, like Paul, was utterly "conquered" by Christ—"*comprehensus sum a Christo Iesu*" ["I have . . . been taken possession of by Christ"] (cf. Phil 3:12)—and like Paul he can exhort the elders with full authority because it is no longer he who lives, but Christ lives in him—"*vivo autem iam non ego, vivit vero in me Christus*" ["yet I live, no longer I, but Christ lives in me"] (Gal 2:20).

Homily at the consistory for the creation of new cardinals
March 24, 2006

26. *Transformation of the "I"*

[Paul says:] You have become one in Christ (cf. Gal 3:28). Not just one thing, but one, one only, one single new subject. This liberation of our "I" from its isolation, this finding oneself in a new subject means finding oneself within the vastness of God and being drawn into a life which has now moved out of the context of "dying and becoming."

Homily at the Easter Vigil
April 15, 2006

27. *Following Christ*

St. Paul . . . assures the Christians of Corinth: "You are in our hearts, to die together and to live together" (2 Cor 7:3). What takes place between the Apostle and his Christians must obviously apply first of all to the relationship between Christians and Jesus himself: dying together, living together, being in his Heart as he is in ours.

General Audience
September 27, 2006

5. The Mystery of the Cross

28. *The scandal of the Cross*

The Mosaic Law was totally fulfilled in Jesus, who revealed God's wisdom and love through the mystery of the Cross, "a stumbling block to Jews and an absurdity to Gentiles; but to those who are called, Jews and Greeks alike, Christ is the power of God and the wisdom of God" (1 Cor 1: 23-24).

Homily on the Feast of St. Joseph
March 19, 2006

29. *The Cross of Christ*

The Apostle Paul says: "We preach Christ crucified, a stumbling block to Jews and folly to Gentiles" (1 Cor 1:23). Christians, however, do not exalt just any cross but the Cross which Jesus sanctified with his sacrifice, the fruit and testimony of immense love.

Angelus
September 17, 2006

30. *Knowledge of the Cross*

The Apostle can affirm that he wants nothing except "Jesus Christ and him crucified" (1 Cor 2:2). It is true: the Cross shows "the breadth and length and height and depth"—the cosmic dimensions is the meaning—of a love that surpasses all knowledge, a love that goes beyond what is known and fills us "with all the fullness of God" (Eph 3:18-19).

General Audience
April 12, 2006

31. *A sign of love*

The manifestation of divine love is total and perfect in the Cross where, we are told by St. Paul, *"God proves his love for us in that while we still were sinners Christ died for us"* (Rom 5:8). Therefore, each one of us can truly say: *"Christ loved me and gave himself up for me"* (cf. Eph 5:2). Redeemed by his blood, no human life is useless or of little value, because each of us is loved personally by Him with a passionate and faithful love, a love without limits.

Message for the Twenty-Second World Youth Day
January 27, 2007

32. *Christ, our peace*

The beauty of the vision described by the Apostle Paul (cf. Eph 2:13-18) is striking: Christ is our peace. He reconciled one to another, Jews and pagans, uniting them in his Body. In his Body, on the Cross, he overcame animosity. He overcame enmity with his death and united us all in his peace.

Prayer service at the Parish of
Rhêmes-Saint Georges, Aosta Valley
July 23, 2006

6. The Way of the Cross

33. The example

In a famous passage from his Letter to the Philippians, the Apostle Paul says that Christ "emptied himself, taking the form of a servant" (Phil 2:7). He, Christ, is the example at which to look. In the Gospel, he told his disciples he had come "not to be served but to serve" (cf. Mt 20:28).

> *Address to the permanent deacons of Rome*
> *February 18, 2006*

34. Kenosis

St. Paul says to all, especially of course to those who work in God's field: "have in yourselves the mind of Christ Jesus" [Phil 2:5]. His mind was such that, faced with the destiny of humanity, he could hardly bear to remain in glory, but had to stoop down and do the incredible, take upon himself the utter poverty of a human life even to the point of suffering on the Cross. This is the mind of Jesus Christ: feeling impelled to bring to humanity the light of the Father, to help us by forming the Kingdom of God with us and in us.

> *Meeting with priests and*
> *permanent deacons of Bavaria*
> *September 14, 2006*

35. *For others*

Referring to Paul's words to the Corinthians, "the love of Christ urges us on" (2 Cor 5:14), I stressed that "the consciousness that, in Christ, God has given himself for us, even unto death, must inspire us to live no longer for ourselves but for him, and, with him, for others" (*God Is Love* [*Deus Caritas Est*], no. 33).

Homily for Ash Wednesday
March 1, 2006

36. *The stigmata*

In the dispute on the right way of seeing and living the Gospel, it is not, in the end, the arguments that decide our thought: it is the reality of life that decides, communion lived and suffered with Jesus, not only in ideas or words but in the depths of our existence, also involving the body, the flesh. The bruises that the Apostle received in the long history of his passion are the witness of the presence of the Cross of Jesus in St. Paul's body; they are his stigmata [see Gal 6:17]. Thus, one can say that it is not circumcision that saves: these stigmata are the consequence of his Baptism, the expression of his dying with Jesus, day after day, the sure sign of his being a new creature.

Homily in Assisi on the eighth centenary
of the conversion of St. Francis
June 17, 2007

7. The Risen One

37. *The joy of Easter*

God's love for us, which began with creation, became visible in the mystery of the Cross, in that *kenosis* of God, in that self-emptying, that abasement of the Son of God which we heard proclaimed . . . in the magnificent hymn to Christ in the Letter to the Philippians [cf. 2:6-11]. Yes, the Cross reveals the fullness of God's love for us. It is a crucified love which does not stop at the scandal of Good Friday but culminates in the joy of the Resurrection.

> *Homily at the penitential celebration for the*
> *youth of the diocese of Rome*
> *March 29, 2007*

38. *Triumph over evil*

Evil in all its forms does not have the last word. The final triumph, the triumph of truth and love, is Christ's! If we are willing to suffer and die with him, St. Paul will remind us . . . his life will become our life (cf. Rom 6:9 ["We know that Christ, raised from the dead, dies no more; death no longer has power over him"]). Our Christian life is supported by and built upon this certainty.

> *General Audience*
> *April 4, 2007*

39. *The fact of the Resurrection*

The Resurrection of Christ is central to Christianity. It is a fundamental truth to be reasserted vigorously in every epoch, since to deny it, as has been, and continues to be attempted, or to transform it into a purely spiritual event, is to thwart our very faith. St. Paul states: "If Christ has not been raised, then our preaching is in vain and your faith is in vain" (1 Cor 15:14).

Regina Caeli
April 30, 2006

40. *The mandate*

In St. Paul's First Letter to the Corinthians, we find the oldest account we have of the Resurrection. Paul faithfully received it from the witnesses. This account first speaks of Christ's death for our sins, of his burial and of his Resurrection which took place the third day, and then says: "[Christ] was seen by Cephas, then by the Twelve . . ."

(1 Cor 15:4). Thus, the importance of the mandate conferred upon Peter to the end of time is summed up: being a witness of the Risen Christ.

> *Homily at the Mass of possession of the*
> *chair of the Bishop of Rome*
> *May 7, 2005*

41. *Witnesses of the Risen One*

"If, then, you have been raised with Christ," St. Paul exhorts us, "seek the things that are above. . . . Set your minds on things that are above, not on things that are on earth" (Col 3:1-2). This does not mean cutting oneself off from one's daily commitments, neglecting earthly realities; rather, it means reviving every human activity with a supernatural breath, it means making ourselves joyful proclaimers and witnesses of the Resurrection of Christ, living for eternity.

> *General Audience*
> *April 19, 2006*

42. *The Lamb of God*

The Cross—for the world a folly, for many believers a scandal—is in fact the "wisdom of God" for those who allow themselves to be touched right to the innermost depths of their being, *"for God's foolishness is wiser than human wisdom, and God's weakness is stronger than human strength"* (1 Cor 1:25). Moreover, the Crucifix, which after the Resurrection would carry forever the marks of his passion, exposes the "distortions" and lies about God that underlie violence, vengeance and exclusion. Christ is the Lamb of God who takes upon himself the sins of the world and eradicates hatred from the heart of humankind. This is the true "revolution" that He brings about: love.

Message for the Twenty-Second World Youth Day
January 27, 2007

III. Life in
the Spirit

8. The Action of the Spirit

43. *Unity*

The Holy Spirit gives understanding. Overcoming the "breach" begun in Babel—the confusion of hearts, putting us one against the other—the Spirit opens borders. The People of God who found its first configuration on Mt. Sinai, now becomes enlarged to the point of recognizing no limitations. . . . St. Paul explains and underlines this . . . when he says: "It was in one Spirit that all of us, whether Jew or Greek, slave or free, were baptized into one body. All of us have been given to drink of the one Spirit" (1 Cor 12:13).

Homily for Mass of Ordination on Pentecost Sunday
May 15, 2005

44. *Blessedness*

We are indeed blessed when the Holy Spirit opens us to the joy of believing and makes us enter the great family of Christians, his Church. For all her rich diversity, in the variety of gifts, ministries and works, the Church is already one, since "it is the same God who inspires them all in every one" [1 Cor 12:4].

> *Homily at the Cathedral of the Holy Spirit, Istanbul*
> *December 1, 2006*

45. *Confession of faith*

As St. Paul has just reminded us ["no one can say, 'Jesus is Lord,' except by the Holy Spirit" (1 Cor 12:3)], the Spirit is the enduring source of our faith and unity. He awakens within us true knowledge of Jesus and he puts on our lips the words of faith that enable us to acknowledge the Lord.

> *Homily at the Cathedral of the Holy Spirit, Istanbul*
> *December 1, 2006*

46. *Life in communion*

[St. Paul says,] "The grace of the Lord Jesus Christ and the love of God and the fellowship of the Holy Spirit be with you all" (2 Cor 13:14). These words, probably echoed in the worship of the newborn Church, emphasize how the free gift of the Father in Jesus Christ is realized and expressed in the communion brought about by the Holy Spirit. . . . communion is also a gift with very real consequences. It lifts us from our loneliness, from being closed in on ourselves, and makes us sharers in the love that unites us to God and to one another.

General Audience
March 29, 2006

47. *The Consoler*

St. Paul again, in the Second Letter to the Corinthians states with conviction that "the God of all consolation . . . comforts us in all our affliction, so that we may be able to comfort those who are in any affliction" (2 Cor 1:3-4). We know well that the consolation promised by the Holy Spirit does not consist merely of nice words, but in a broadening of mind and heart, that allows us to understand our own situation in the wider picture of all creation laboring in the act of giving birth while awaiting the revelation of the . . . [children] of God (cf. Rom 8:19-25).

Christmas message to Catholics living in the Middle East
December 21, 2006

9. The Spirit in Our Hearts

48. *The indwelling of the Spirit*

In Paul's reflection on the Spirit he not only explained his influence on the *action* of Christians, but also on their *being*. Indeed, it is he who said that the Spirit of God dwells in us (cf. Rom 8:9; 1 Cor 3:16) and that "God has sent the Spirit of his Son into our hearts" (Gal 4:6).

General Audience
November 15, 2006

49. *The Spirit of Jesus*

St. Paul spoke directly of the "Spirit of Christ" (Rom 8:9), of the "Spirit of his Son" (cf. Gal 4:6) or of the "Spirit of Jesus Christ" (Phil 1:19). It is as though he wanted to say that not only is God the Father visible in the Son (cf. Jn 14:9), but that the Spirit of God also expresses himself in the life and action of the Crucified and Risen Lord!

General Audience
November 15, 2006

50. *Prayer and the Spirit*

Paul teaches us another important thing: he says that there is no true prayer without the presence of the Spirit within us. He wrote: "The Spirit helps us in our weakness; for we do not know how to pray as we ought, but the Spirit himself intercedes for us with sighs too deep for words . . ." (Rom 8:26-27). . . . It is an invitation to be increasingly sensitive, more attentive to this presence of the Spirit in us, to transform it into prayer, to feel this presence and thus to learn to pray, to speak to the Father as children in the Holy Spirit.

General Audience
November 15, 2006

51. *Manifesting the Spirit*

St. Paul adds that: "to each is given the manifestation of the Spirit for the common good" [1 Cor 12:70]. To manifest the Spirit, to live by the Spirit, is not to live for oneself alone, but to let oneself be conformed to Christ Jesus by becoming, like him, the servant of his brothers and sisters.

Homily at the Cathedral of the Holy Spirit, Istanbul
December 1, 2006

52. *Our inheritance*

According to St. Paul, the Spirit is a generous down payment given to us by God himself as a deposit and at the same time, a guarantee of our future inheritance (cf. 2 Cor 1:22; 5:5; Eph 1:13-14).

General Audience
November 15, 2006

10. Adoption as Sons and Daughters

53. *Divine adoption*

The Apostle Paul writes: "Blessed be the God and Father of our Lord Jesus Christ . . . even as he chose us in him before the foundation of the world. . . . He destined us in love to be his sons through Jesus Christ" (Eph 1:3-5). Before the creation of the world, before our coming into existence, the heavenly Father chose us personally, calling us to enter into a filial relationship with Him, through Jesus, the Incarnate Word, under the guidance of the Holy Spirit.

Message for the Forty-Third World Day of
Prayer for Vocations
March 5, 2006

54. *Children of God thanks to the Spirit*

[St. Paul says,] "You did not receive the spirit of slavery to fall back into fear, but you have received the spirit of sonship. When we cry, 'Abba! Father!', it is the Spirit himself" (Rom 8:2, 15) who speaks in us because, as children, we can call God "Father." This is our greatest dignity: to be not merely images but also children of God. And it is an invitation to live our sonship, to be increasingly aware that we are adoptive sons in God's great family.

General Audience
November 15, 2006

55. *Filial responsibility*

The Holy Spirit . . . makes us sons and daughters of God [says St. Paul (cf. Rom 8:15)]. He involves us in the same responsibility that God has for his world, for the whole of humanity. He teaches us to look at the world, others and ourselves with God's eyes. We do not do good as slaves who are not free to act otherwise, but we do it because we are personally responsible for the world; because we love truth and goodness, because we love God himself and therefore, also his creatures. This is the true freedom to which the Holy Spirit wants to lead us.

Homily on the Vigil of Pentecost
June 3, 2006

11. Freedom

56. Freedom of the children of God

We want the true, great freedom, the freedom of heirs, the freedom of children of God [cf. Rom 8:15]. In this world, so full of fictitious forms of freedom that destroy the environment and the human being, let us learn true freedom by the power of the Holy Spirit; to build the school of freedom; to show others by our lives that we are free and how beautiful it is to be truly free with the true freedom of God's children.

Homily on the Vigil of Pentecost
June 3, 2006

57. Freedom from sin

Paul says . . . that "God sent forth his Son . . . to redeem those who were under the law, so that we might receive adoption as sons" (Gal 4:4-5). The Incarnate Word transforms human life from within, sharing with us his being as Son of the Father. He became like us in order for us to become like him: children of the Son, hence, people free from the law of sin.

Homily at First Vespers, Vigil of the
Solemnity of Mary, Mother of God
December 31, 2007

58. *Freedom as service*

[St. Paul writes:] "You were called to freedom, brethren; only do not use your freedom as an opportunity for the flesh, but through love be servants of one another" (Gal 5:13). Freedom is mutual service.

Meeting with the diplomatic corps to
the Republic of Turkey
November 28, 2006

IV. The Christian Experience

59. *Definition*

[St. Paul addresses] all who are distinguished in the world by the fact that they "call on the name of Our Lord Jesus Christ" (1 Cor 1:2). This is our definition: we belong among those who call on the Name of the Lord Jesus Christ.

General Audience
November 22, 2006

12. The Sentiments of Jesus

60. *The right path*

I want to underline . . . this admonition of St. Paul: "Have this mind among yourselves, which was in Christ Jesus" [Phil 2:5]. To learn to feel as Jesus felt; to conform our way of thinking, deciding and acting to the sentiments of Jesus. We will take up this path if we look to conform our sentiments to those of Jesus. Let us take up the right path.

General Audience
October 26, 2005

61. *Familiarity*

In Paul's Letter to the Ephesians, one [reads] that what is important is to "learn Christ" (Eph 4:20): therefore, not only and not so much to listen to his teachings and words as rather to know him in person, that is, his humanity and his divinity, his mystery and his beauty. In fact, he is not only a Teacher but a Friend, indeed, a Brother. How will we be able to get to know him properly by being distant? Closeness, familiarity and habit make us discover the true identity of Jesus Christ.

General Audience
September 6, 2006

62. *Friendship with Jesus*

Friendship means sharing in thought and will. We must put into practice this communion of thought with Jesus, as St. Paul tells us in his Letter to the Philippians (cf. Phil 2:2-5). And this communion of thought is not a purely intellectual thing, but a sharing of sentiments and will, hence, also of actions. This means that we should know Jesus in an increasingly personal way, listening to him, living together with him, staying with him.

> *Homily for Chrism Mass in St. Peter's Basilica*
> *Holy Thursday, April 13, 2006*

63. *Thinking with the heart*

St. Paul cries to us in God's Name: "Your attitude must be Christ's—*Touto phroneite en hymin ho kai en Christo Iesou*" [Phil 2:5]. Learn to think as Christ thought, learn to think with him! And this thinking is not only the thinking of the mind, but also a thinking of the heart.

> *Homily at Mass with the members of the*
> *Bishops' Conference of Switzerland*
> *November 7, 2006*

64. *True progress*

"In him [and for him] all things were created . . ." (cf. Col 1:16-17). . . . And so St. Paul points out to us a very important truth: history has a destination, a direction. History moves toward humanity united in Christ and thus moves in the direction of the perfect man, toward the perfect humanism.

General Audience
January 4, 2006

65. *The new spirit*

[We should have] the new spirit of those who have found the meaning of life in Jesus and in his Paschal Mystery and realize that henceforth everything must refer to him. This was the attitude of the Apostle Paul who affirmed that he had left everything behind in order to know Christ [cf. Phil 3:7].

Angelus
February 26, 2006

13. The Fruits of the Spirit

66. *Love*

It is not without significance that when Paul lists the various elements that constitute the fruit of the Spirit he puts love first: "the fruit of the Spirit is love, joy, peace," etc. (Gal 5:22). . . . the Spirit stimulates us to weave charitable relations with all people. Therefore, when we love we make room for the Spirit and give him leeway to express himself fully within us.

General Audience
November 15, 2006

67. *Concord*

The Apostle, aware of how easy it is to succumb to the ever latent threat of conflicts and disputes, urged the young Community at Philippi to concord and unity. To the Galatians he was to indicate forcefully that the whole law finds its fullness in the one precept of love; and he exhorts them to proceed in accordance with the Spirit so as to avoid acts of the flesh—discord, jealousy, disagreement, division, factions, envy—and thus to obtain instead the fruit of the Spirit which is love (cf. Gal 5:14-23).

Address to the delegation of the ecumenical
patriarchate of Constantinople
June 30, 2005

68. *Fraternal correction*

["Encourage one another," writes Paul (2 Cor 13:11).] Fraternal correction is a work of mercy. None of us sees himself or his shortcomings clearly. It is therefore an act of love to complement one another, to help one another see each other better, and correct each other.

> *Reflection at the Eleventh Ordinary General*
> *Assembly of the Synod of Bishops*
> *October 3, 2005*

69. *Generosity*

It is wisdom and virtue not to set one's heart on the goods of this world for all things are transient, all things can suddenly end. For us Christians, the real treasure that we must ceaselessly seek consists in the "things above . . . where Christ is seated at God's right hand" [Col 3:1-3].

> *Angelus*
> *August 5, 2007*

70. *Joy*

"Gaudete, iterum dico gaudete quia Dominus prope est." ["Rejoice in the Lord always; again I say, rejoice! The Lord is near" (Phil 4:4-5).] Here we understand the reason why Paul, in all his sufferings, in all his trials, could only tell others to "rejoice"; he could say this because joy was present

within him. . . . If the loved one, the love, the greatest gift of my life, is close to me; if I can be convinced that the person who loves me is beside me even in troubling situations, in the depths of my heart dwells a joy that is greater than all suffering. The Apostle could say "be happy" because the Lord is close to each one of us.

Reflection at the Eleventh Ordinary General
Assembly of the Synod of Bishops
October 3, 2005

71. *Perseverance*

Perseverance in good, even if it is misunderstood and opposed, always reaches a landing place of light, fruitfulness and peace. This is what St. Paul reminded the Galatians: ". . . if his seed-ground is the spirit, he will reap everlasting life. Let us not grow weary of doing good; if we do not relax our efforts, in due time we shall reap our harvest" (Gal 6:8-9).

General Audience
August 17, 2005

72. *Inner peace*

["Live in peace," says St. Paul (2 Cor 13:11).] Only if we are grounded in deep inner peace can we also be men and women of peace in the world and for others.

> *Reflection at the Eleventh Ordinary General*
> *Assembly of the Synod of Bishops*
> *October 3, 2005*

73. *The Kingdom of God*

We find one of the most beautiful definitions of the Kingdom of God in . . . the Letter to the Romans. The Apostle Paul, after urging Christians always to allow themselves to be guided by love and not to be objects of scandal for those who are weak in faith, recalls that the Kingdom of God is "righteousness and peace and joy in the Holy Spirit" (Rom 14:17).

> *Homily for the 500th anniversary of the*
> *founding of the Pontifical Swiss Guard Corps*
> *May 6, 2006*

14. "So Faith, Hope, Love Remain, These Three; but the Greatest of These Is Love" (1 Cor 13:13)

FAITH

74. *Believing*

[St. Paul writes that] God has given us a spirit of wisdom and "enlightened the eyes of our hearts, that we may know what is the hope to which he has called us, the riches of his glorious inheritance in the saints, and the immeasurable greatness of his power in us who believe, according to the working of his great power in Christ" (cf. Eph 1:17-20). Believing means surrendering ourselves to God and entrusting our destiny to him. Believing means entering into a personal relationship with our Creator and Redeemer in the power of the Holy Spirit, and making this relationship the basis of our whole life.

Homily at Mass in Krakow, Poland
May 28, 2006

75. *In the Lord's hands*

We must be sure that however burdensome and tempestuous the trials that await us may be, we will never be left on our own, we will never fall out of the Lord's hands, those hands that created us and now sustain us on our journey through life. As St. Paul was to confess: "he who has begun the good work in you will carry it through to completion" (Phil 1:6).

General Audience
December 7, 2005

76. *Optimism*

Jesus, the Good Shepherd, acts in souls with his grace. *"My grace is sufficient for you"* (2 Cor 12:9), the Apostle Paul heard the Lord answer when he asked the Lord to spare him suffering. May this very awareness always nourish your faith and stimulate within you the search for ways to reach the hearts of all with the healthy optimism that you must always spread around you.

Address to newly ordained bishops
September 21, 2006

77. *Trust*

Even in the darkest moments of our lives, we know that God is never absent. St. Paul reminds us that "in everything God works for good with those who love him" (Rom 8:28).

> *Address to the bishops of Sri Lanka*
> *on their* ad limina *visit*
> *May 7, 2005*

HOPE

78. *Receiving hope*

Paul reminds the Ephesians that before their encounter with Christ they were "without hope and without God in the world" (Eph 2:12). . . . To come to know God—the true God—means to receive hope.

Encyclical letter On Christian Hope (Spe Salvi), *no. 3*
November 30, 2007

79. *Christian hope*

[Paul] says to the Thessalonians: you must not "grieve as others do who have no hope" (1 Thes 4:13). Here too we see as a distinguishing mark of Christians the fact that they have a future: it is not that they know the details of what awaits them, but they know in general terms that their life will not end in emptiness. Only when the future is certain as a positive reality does it become possible to live the present as well.

Encyclical letter On Christian Hope (Spe Salvi), *no. 2*
November 30, 2007

80. *Building hope*

We need to build up hope, weaving the fabric of a society that, by relaxing its grip on the threads of life, is losing the true sense of hope. This loss, according to St. Paul, is the self-imposed curse of "heartless persons" (Rom 1:31).

Meeting with the Poor Clares in Brazil
May 12, 2007

81. *Rootedness*

The hope of Christians is turned to the future but remains firmly rooted in an event of the past. In the fullness of time, the Son of God was born of the Virgin Mary: "Born of a woman, born under the law," as the Apostle Paul writes (Gal 4:4).

Angelus
November 27, 2005

CHARITY

82. *Proclamation*

For Christians . . . the words of St. Paul are valid: "The love of Christ impels us" (2 Cor 5:14). The charity that moved the Father to send his Son into the world, and moved the Son to offer himself for us even to death on the Cross, that same charity has been poured out by the Holy Spirit in the hearts of believers. Every baptized person, as a vine united to the branch, can therefore cooperate in the mission of Jesus, which can be summarized thus: to bring to every person the good news that "God is love" and, precisely for this reason, wants to save the world.

Angelus
October 22, 2006

83. *Self-giving*

St. Paul, in his hymn to charity (cf. 1 Cor 13), teaches us that it is always more than activity alone: "If I give away all I have, and if I deliver my body to be burned, but do not have love, I gain nothing" (1 Cor 13:3). . . . Practical activity will always be insufficient, unless it visibly expresses a love for man, a love nourished by an encounter with Christ. My deep personal sharing in the needs and sufferings of others becomes a sharing of my very self with them: if my gift is not to prove a source of humiliation, I must give to others not only something that is my own, but my very self; I must be personally present in my gift.

Encyclical letter God Is Love (Deus Caritas Est), *no. 34*
December 25, 2005

84. *God is love*

I am convinced that humanity today stands in need of this essential message, incarnate in Jesus Christ: God is love. Everything must start from here and everything must lead to here, every pastoral action, every theological treatise. As St. Paul said, "If I . . . have not love I gain nothing" (cf. 1 Cor 13:3). All charisms lose their meaning and value without love, thanks to which instead, all compete to build the Mystical Body of Christ.

Homily at Vespers in Pavia, Italy
April 22, 2007

85. *Unconditional love*

The human being needs unconditional love. He needs the certainty which makes him say: "neither death, nor life, nor angels, nor principalities, nor things present, nor things to come, nor powers, nor height, nor depth, nor anything else in all creation, will be able to separate us from the love of God in Christ Jesus our Lord" (Rom 8:38-39). If this absolute love exists, with its absolute certainty, then—only then—is man "redeemed," whatever should happen to him in his particular circumstances.

Encyclical letter On Christian Hope (Spe Salvi), *no. 26*
November 30, 2007

86. *Justice and charity*

Justice alone is insufficient to establish truly humane and fraternal relations within society. . . . [As St. Paul proclaims, love "is patient and kind" (1 Cor 13:4).] Charity, in a word, not only enables justice to become more inventive and to meet new challenges; it also inspires and purifies humanity's efforts to achieve authentic justice and thus the building of a society worthy of man.

Letter to Professor Mary Ann Glendon
for the Thirteenth Plenary Session of
the Pontifical Academy for the Sciences
April 28, 2007

87. *Missionaries of love*

St. Paul, the Apostle to the Gentiles, wrote: "The love of Christ impels us" (2 Cor 5:14). May every Christian make these words his own, in the joyful experience of being a missionary of Love wherever Providence has placed him, with humility and courage, serving his neighbor with no ulterior motives and drawing strength from prayer for a cheerful and industrious charity.

Angelus
October 1, 2006

15. Faith and Works

88. *The Christian's faith*

[Paul] wrote in his *Letter to the Romans:* "We hold that a man is justified by faith apart from works of law" (Rom 3:28). . . . Paul states with absolute clarity that this condition of life does not depend on our possible good works but on the pure grace of God: "[We] are justified by his grace as a gift, through the redemption which is in Christ Jesus" (Rom 3:24).

General Audience
November 8, 2006

89. *Justification*

Paul . . . claims that we are justified by God not by virtue of our actions but through our faith (cf. Gal 2:16; Rom 3:28). St. Paul is opposed to the pride of man who thinks he does not need the love of God that precedes us; he is opposed to the pride of self-justification without grace, simply given and undeserved.

General Audience
June 28, 2006

90. *Law and grace*

The Wisdom of God is contained in the Decalogue. This is why Jesus affirms in the Gospel that to "enter into life" it is necessary to observe the commandments (cf. Mk 10:19). It is necessary, but not sufficient! In fact, as St. Paul says, salvation does not come from the law, but from Grace.

Mass for the canonization of Rafael Guizar Valencia,
Filippio Smaldone, Rosa Venerini, and Theodore Guerin
October 15, 2006

16. Conversion

91. *Human weakness*

In order to respond to the call of God and start on our journey, it is not necessary to be already perfect. . . . Weaknesses and human limitations do not present an obstacle, as long as they help make us more aware of the fact that we are in need of the redeeming grace of Christ. This is the experience of St. Paul who confessed: "I will all the more gladly boast of my weaknesses, that the power of Christ may rest upon me" (2 Cor 12:9). In the mystery of the Church, the mystical Body of Christ, the divine power of love changes the heart of man, making him able to communicate the love of God to his brothers and sisters.

> *Message for the Forty-Third World Day of*
> *Prayer for Vocations*
> *March 5, 2006*

92. *The journey*

[As St. Paul wrote to the Thessalonians,] "You turned to God from idols, to serve him who is the living and true God" (1 Thes 1:9). This conversion is the beginning of the walk of holiness that the Christian is called to achieve in his own life. The saint is the person who is so fascinated by the beauty of God and by his perfect truth as to be progressively transformed by it. Because of this beauty and truth, he is ready to renounce everything, even himself. Love of God is enough for him, experienced in humble and disinterested service to one's neighbor, especially towards those who cannot give back in return.

Homily for World Missions Day
October 23, 2005

17. Sanctification

93. *Communion in Christ*

St. Paul reminds us that through Christ we are no longer strangers and aliens but citizens with the saints and members of the household of God, growing into a holy temple, a dwelling place for God (cf. Eph. 2:19-22). This sublime portrayal of a life of communion engages all aspects of our lives as Christians.

Address to the Pontifical Council for
Social Communications
March 17, 2006

94. *Strive for perfection* (cf. 2 Cor 13:11)

[The words of St. Paul] invite us to be what we are: images of God, beings created in relation to the Lord, "mirrors" where the Lord's light is reflected. Not to live Christianity according to the letter, not to understand Sacred Scripture according to the letter is often difficult, historically disputable; but we must go beyond the letter, our present reality, towards the Lord who speaks to us and hence, to union with God.

Reflection at the Eleventh Ordinary
General Assembly of the Synod of Bishops
October 3, 2005

95. *Universal holiness*

In his First Letter to the Corinthians, St. Paul addresses "those sanctified in Christ Jesus, called to be saints together with all those who in every place call on the name of our Lord Jesus Christ" (1 Cor 1:2). Indeed, Christians are already saints because Baptism unites them to Jesus and to his Paschal Mystery, but at the same time they must become so by conforming themselves ever more closely to him.

Angelus
November 1, 2007

96. *Called*

All men and women, according to St. Paul, are called to be holy and blameless in God's sight, full of love (cf. Eph 1:4-5).

Angelus
December 8, 2005

97. *Holiness*

To become saints means to completely fulfill what we already are, raised to the dignity of God's adopted children, in Christ Jesus (cf. Eph 1:5; Rom 8:14-17).

Angelus
November 1, 2005

V. THE CHURCH OF GOD

98. *Love, the heart of the Church*

My venerable predecessor Pope John Paul II stated that ". . . Many things are necessary for the Church's journey through history, not least in this new century; but without charity (*agape*) all will be in vain. It is again the Apostle Paul who in his *hymn to love* reminds us: even if we speak the tongues of men and of angels, and if we have faith 'to move mountains,' but are without love, all will come to 'nothing' (cf. 1 Cor 13:2). Love is truly the 'heart' of the Church."

Letter to the faithful of China
May 27, 2007

18. People of God, Body of Christ, Temple of God

99. *Sign of unity*

Paul knows that he has been sent to proclaim a "mystery," a divine plan that only in the fullness of time has been carried out and revealed in Christ: namely, that "the Gentiles have become fellow heirs, members of the same body, and sharers in the promise in Christ Jesus through the Gospel" (Eph 3:6). This *mystery* is accomplished, in salvation history, *in the Church*, the new People in which, now that the old dividing wall has been broken down, Jews and pagans find themselves united. Like Christ himself, the Church is not only the *instrument* of unity, but also its *efficacious sign*.

Homily in Ephesus during his
apostolic journey to Turkey
November 29, 2006

100. *The centrality of the Church*

For Paul, adherence to the Church was brought about by a direct intervention of Christ, who in revealing himself on the road to Damascus identified himself with the Church and made Paul realize that persecution of the Church was persecution of himself, the Lord. In fact, the Risen One said to Paul, persecutor of the Church: "Saul, Saul, why do you persecute me?" (Acts 9:4). In persecuting the Church, he was persecuting Christ. Paul, therefore, was at the same time converted to Christ and to the Church. This leads one to understand why the Church later became so present in Paul's thoughts, heart and activity.

General Audience
November 22, 2006

101. *Christ and the Church*

On the road to Damascus, Saul hears the disturbing question: "Why do you persecute me?" Falling to the ground and interiorly troubled, he asked: "Who are you, Lord?", receiving that answer which is the basis of his conversion: "I am Jesus, whom you are persecuting" (Acts 9:4-5). Paul understood in an instant what he would later express in his writings: that the Church forms a single body of which Christ is the Head. And so, from a persecutor of Christians he became the Apostle to the Gentiles.

Homily at the Basilica of St. Paul Outside-the-Walls
January 25, 2006

102. *The mystical body*

Paul makes us understand that not only does the belonging of the Church to Christ exist, but also a certain form of equality and identification of the Church with Christ himself. From this, therefore, derive the greatness and nobility of the Church, that is, of all of us who are part of her: from our being members of Christ, an extension as it were of his personal presence in the world.

General Audience
November 22, 2006

103. *Charisms in the Christian community*

Underlining the need for unity does not mean that ecclesial life should be standardized or leveled out in accordance with a single way of operating. Elsewhere, Paul taught: "Do not quench the Spirit" (1 Thes 5:19), that is, make room generously for the unforeseeable dynamism of the charismatic manifestations of the Spirit, who is an ever new source of energy and vitality.

General Audience
November 22, 2006

104. *Do not extinguish charisms*

St. Paul in his First Letter to the Thessalonians [teaches us]: do not extinguish charisms [cf. 1 Thes 5:19]. If the Lord gives us new gifts we must be grateful, even if at times they may be inconvenient. And it is beautiful that without an initiative of the hierarchy but with an initiative from below, as people say, but which also truly comes from on High, that is, as a gift of the Holy Spirit, new forms of life are being born in the Church just as, moreover, they were born down the ages.

Lenten meeting with the clergy of Rome
February 22, 2007

105. *Bride of Christ*

There is also a Pauline Letter that presents the Church as Christ's Bride (cf. Eph 5:21-33). . . . He did so to express the intimacy of the relationship between Christ and his Church, both in the sense that she is the object of the most tender love on the part of her Lord, and also in the sense that love must be mutual and that we too therefore, as members of the Church, must show him passionate faithfulness.

General Audience
November 22, 2006

106. *Holy City*

Just as in their love man and woman become "one flesh," so Christ and humanity gathered in the Church become through Christ's love "one spirit" (cf. 1 Cor 6:17; Eph 5:29ff.). Paul calls Christ the new, the last Adam: definitive man. And he calls him "a life-giving spirit" (1 Cor 15:45). With him, we become one; with him, the Church becomes a life-giving spirit. The holy City, where there is no longer a temple because it is inhabited by God, is the image of this community that is formed from Christ.

Homily at Our Lady Star of Evangelization Parish, Rome
December 10, 2006

107. *Spiritual body*

Although she is a body, the Church is the Body of Christ, hence, she is a spiritual body, as St. Paul said. She is a spiritual reality. I think this is very important: that people see that the Church is not a supranational organization nor an administrative body or power, that she is not a social agency, but indeed that although she does social and supranational work, she is a spiritual body.

Lenten meeting with the clergy of Rome
February 22, 2007

108. *Family of God*

Not by chance does Paul compare, in the *Letter to the Ephesians,* the matrimonial relationship to the spousal communion that happens between Christ and the Church (cf. Eph 5:25-33). Even more, we can maintain that the Apostle indirectly models the life of the entire Church on that of the family. And the Church, in reality, is the family of God.

General Audience
February 7, 2007

109. *The Holy Spirit and the Church*

St. Paul's doctrine reveals a very special power, obviously founded on divine revelation but also on his own apostolic experience, which confirmed anew the awareness that not wisdom and human eloquence, but only the power of the Holy Spirit builds the Church in the faith [cf. 1 Cor 1:22-24; 2:4ff.].

Address to the General Secretariat of
the Synod of Bishops
January 21, 2008

19. Unity and Dialogue Between the Churches

110. *Ecumenical dialogue*

This is very important: we must tolerate the separation that exists. St. Paul says that divisions are necessary for a certain time and that the Lord knows why: to test us, to train us, to develop us, to make us more humble [cf. 1 Cor 11:19]. But at the same time, we are obliged to move towards unity, and moving towards unity is already a form of unity.

Address to the Roman clergy
March 2, 2006

111. *Unity*

In the first chapter of the Letter to the Christians of Corinth, who were the first to experience the problems and grave temptations of division, we can see a timely message for all Christians. Indeed, a real danger appears when people prefer to identify with one group rather than another, saying, "I belong to Paul" or "I belong to Apollos," or "I belong to Cephas." It was then that Paul asked the searching question. "Is Christ divided?" (1 Cor 1:13).

Address to the Archbishop of Athens and Greece
December 14, 2006

112. *Need for prayer*

"Pray without ceasing" (1 Thes 5:17). St. Paul addressed the community of Thessalonica, which was experiencing inner disputes and conflicts, in order to appeal forcefully for certain fundamental attitudes, among which stands out ceaseless prayer. With this invitation, he wanted to make people understand that the capacity to overcome all selfishness, to live together in peace and fraternal union and for each one to bear the burdens and suffering of others comes from new life in Christ and in the Holy Spirit. We must never tire of praying for Christian unity!

Angelus
January 20, 2008

113. *Ecumenical relations*

The advice that St. Paul gave to the Thessalonians can still inspire the behavior of Christians in the context of ecumenical relations today. Above all he said: "Be at peace among yourselves," and then, "pray constantly, give thanks in all circumstances" (1 Thes 5:13, 18). Let us also accept the Apostle's pressing exhortation, both to thank the Lord for the progress achieved and to implore full unity.

General Audience
January 23, 2008

20. Proclaiming the Gospel

114. *Preaching*

In the words of the Apostle of the Gentiles, . . . our Savior *"desires all men to be saved and to come to the knowledge of the truth"* (1 Tm 2:4). This, and nothing else, is the purpose of the Church: the salvation of individual souls. For this reason the Father sent his Son, and in the Lord's own words transmitted to us in the Gospel of St. John, *"as the Father has sent me, even so I send you"* (Jn 20:21). Hence the mandate to preach the Gospel.

> *Homily at Vespers with the bishops of Brazil*
> *May 11, 2007*

115. *The message*

The Church's task is none other than to spread the message of Christ, who came, as St. Paul writes in the Letter to the Ephesians, to proclaim peace to those who are far away and to those who are near (cf. Eph 2:17).

> *Address to the diplomatic corps*
> *accredited to the Holy See*
> *January 9, 2006*

116. *Faith comes from hearing*

Faith, as knowledge and profession of the truth about God and about man, "comes from what is heard, and what is heard comes by the preaching of Christ," as St. Paul says (Rom 10:17)

Homily in Piłsudzki Square, Poland
May 26, 2006

117. *Faith and culture*

The Christian faith is open to "whatever is true, honorable, just, pure, lovely, gracious" in the culture of peoples, as the Apostle Paul taught the Philippians (cf. Phil 4:8).

Address to the media of the Italian bishops' conference
June 2, 2006

118. *Biblical faith and Greek inquiry*

The vision of St. Paul, who saw the roads to Asia barred and in a dream saw a Macedonian man plead with him: "Come over to Macedonia and help us!" (cf. Acts 16: 6-10)—this vision can be interpreted as a "distillation" of the intrinsic necessity of a rapprochement between Biblical faith and Greek inquiry.

Lecture at the University of Regensburg
September 12, 2006

119. *At the Areopagus*

St. Paul, at the Areopagus in Athens . . . had made the first attempt at dialogue with Greek philosophy—and by and large had failed—but they said to him: "We will hear you again."

General Audience
April 18, 2007

120. *Evangelization*

The work of evangelization is never a simple adaptation to culture, but it is always also a purification, a courageous break that leads to maturation and healing, an openness that brings to birth that "new creation" (2 Cor 5:17; Gal 6:15) which is the fruit of the Holy Spirit.

Address at the Fourth National
Ecclesial Convention, Verona
October 19, 2006

121. *Faithfulness* (1)

To the Lord, whom he first persecuted and then to whom he consecrated his entire being, Paul remains faithful even to death. May his example be an encouragement for all to accept the Word of salvation and translate it into daily life through the faithful following of Christ.

Address to the General Secretariat of
the Synod of Bishops
January 21, 2008

122. *Faithfulness* (2)

St. Paul, it is well-known, originally called by Christ with a personal vocation, was a real Apostle, yet for him too, fidelity to what he received was fundamentally important. He did not want "to invent" a new, so-to-speak, "Pauline" Christianity. Therefore, he insisted, "I have passed on to you what I too received" [1 Cor 15:3]. He passed on the initial gift that comes from the Lord and the truth that saves. Then, towards the end of his life, he wrote to Timothy: "Guard this rich trust with the help of the Holy Spirit that dwells within us" (2 Tm 1:14).

General Audience
May 3, 2006

123. *Vocation and mission*

The story of Paul, the greatest missionary of all times, brings out in many ways the link between vocation and mission. Accused by his opponents of not being authorized for the apostolate, he makes repeated appeals precisely to the call which he received directly from the Lord (cf. Rom 1:1; Gal 1:11-12, 15-17).

> *Message for the Forty-Fifth World Day of*
> *Prayer for Vocations*
> *December 3, 2007*

124. *Peter and Paul*

From the outset, Christian tradition has considered Peter and Paul to have been inseparable, even if each had a different mission to accomplish. Peter professed his faith in Christ first; Paul obtained as a gift the ability to deepen its riches. Peter founded the first community of Christians who came from the Chosen People; Paul became the Apostle to the Gentiles. With different charisms they worked for one and the same cause: the building of Christ's Church.

> *Homily at First Vespers, Solemnity of SS. Peter and Paul*
> *June 28, 2007*

125. *The task*

The Church of the third millennium proposes to offer Christians the capacity for "knowledge [according to the words of St. Paul] . . . of God's mystery, of Christ, in whom are hid all the treasures of wisdom and knowledge" (Col 2:2-3).

Address at the Shrine of Aparecida
May 12, 2007

21. Sacred Ministers

126. *The Church's "joints"*

In his Letter to the Ephesians, St. Paul tell us that this Body of Christ, which is the Church, has joints (cf. Eph 4:16) and even names them: they are apostles, prophets, evangelists, pastors and teachers (cf. 4:12).

Homily on the Vigil of Pentecost
June 3, 2006

127. *The bishop*

As you take your first steps in the episcopal office, you have already realized the great need for humble trust in God and for the apostolic courage that is born from the faith and from the Bishop's sense of responsibility. The Apostle Paul knew this; in setting about his pastoral work he placed his hope in the Lord alone, recognizing that his power came only from the Lord. Indeed, he said: "In him who is the source of my strength I have strength for everything"

(Phil 4:13). Each one of you, dear Brothers, must have the assurance that in carrying out your ministry you are never alone, for the Lord is close to you with his grace and his presence.

Address to newly appointed bishops
September 19, 2005

128. *Commissioned*

The Risen Lord himself called Paul (cf. Gal 1:1), but Paul, although he was called by the Lord to be an Apostle, compared his Gospel with the Gospel of the Twelve (cf. ibid., 1:18), and was concerned to transmit what he had received (cf. 1 Cor 11:23; 15:3-4). In the distribution of missionary tasks, he was associated with the Apostles together with others, for example, Barnabas (cf. Gal 2:9). Just as becoming an Apostle begins with being called and sent out by the Risen One, so the subsequent call and sending out to others was to be brought about, through the power of the Spirit, by those who are already ordained in the apostolic ministry.

General Audience
May 10, 2006

129. *Portrait of the priest*

The Apostle Paul's words can apply to us: "Yet preaching the Gospel is not the subject of a boast; I am under compulsion and have no choice. I am ruined if I do not preach it! . . . Although I am not bound to anyone, I made myself the slave of all so as to win over as many as possible. . . . I have made myself all things to all men in order to save at least some of them" (1 Cor 9:16-22). These words that are the self-portrait of the Apostle are also the portrait of every priest. Making oneself "all things to all men" is expressed in daily life, in attention to every person and family.

Address to the clergy of Rome
May 13, 2005

130. *The priest's mission*

Jesus Christ was sent by the Father, through the power of the Holy Spirit, for the salvation of the entire human family, and we priests are enabled through the grace of the sacrament to share in this mission of his. As the Apostle Paul writes, "God . . . has given us the ministry of reconciliation. . . . This makes us ambassadors for Christ, God as it were appealing through us. We implore you, in Christ's name: be reconciled to God" (2 Cor 5:18-29). This is how St. Paul describes our mission as priests.

Address to the clergy of Rome
May 13, 2005

131. *Bringing God*

Paul calls Timothy . . . "man of God" (1 Tm 6:11). This is the central task of the priest: to bring God to men and women. Of course, he can only do this if he himself comes from God, if he lives *with* and *by* God.

> *Christmas greetings to the Roman Curia*
> *December 22, 2006*

22. The Faithful

132. *Paul and his collaborators*

In carrying out his missions, Paul availed himself of collaborators. He certainly remains the Apostle par excellence, founder and pastor of many Churches. Yet it clearly appears that he did not do everything on his own but relied on trustworthy people who shared in his endeavors and responsibilities. . . . This also seems important to me. Paul does not act as a "soloist," on his own, but together with these collaborators in the "we" of the Church. This "I" of Paul is not an isolated "I" but an "I" in the "we" of the Church, in the "we" of the apostolic faith.

General Audiences
December 13, 2006, and January 31, 2007

133. *The apostolate*

It is necessary to go to the very fringes of society to take to everyone the light of Christ's message about the meaning of life, the family and society, reaching out to those who live in the desert of neglect and poverty and loving them with the love of the Risen Christ. In every apostolate and in Gospel proclamation, as St. Paul says, "If I . . . have not love, I am nothing" (1 Cor 13:2).

Address to pilgrims from Madrid
July 4, 2005

134. *Women in the Church*

It is . . . to St. Paul that we are indebted for a more ample documentation on the dignity and ecclesial role of women. He begins with the fundamental principle according to which for the baptized: "There is neither Jew nor Greek, there is neither slave nor free, there is neither male nor female; for you are all one in Christ Jesus" (Gal 3:28), that is, all are united in the same basic dignity, although each with specific functions (cf. 1 Cor 12:27-30). The Apostle accepts as normal the fact that a woman can "prophesy" in the Christian community (1 Cor 11:5), that is, speak openly under the influence of the Spirit, as long as it is for the edification of the community and done in a dignified manner.

General Audience
February 14, 2007

135. *Humble ministers*

Let us think again of St. Paul's phrase: both Apollos and I are servants of Jesus, each one in his own way because it is God who gives the growth [cf. 1 Cor 3:5-9]. These words also apply to us today, to the Pope, the Cardinals, Bishops, priests and laity. We are all humble ministers of Jesus. We serve the Gospel as best we can, in accordance with our talents, and we pray God to make his Gospel, his Church, increase in our day.

General Audience
January 31, 2007

VI. THE SACRAMENTS

23. Baptism

136. *Washing of regeneration*

St. Paul tells us: "He saved us, not because of deeds done by us in righteousness, but in virtue of his own mercy, by the washing of regeneration and renewal in the Holy Spirit" (Ti 3:5). . . . Baptism is not only a word, it is not only something spiritual but also implies matter. All the realities of the earth are involved. Baptism does not only concern the soul. Human spirituality invests the totality of the person, body and soul. God's action in Jesus Christ is an action of universal efficacy. Christ took flesh and this continues in the sacraments in which matter is taken on and becomes part of the divine action.

> *Homily at Mass and Baptisms in the Sistine Chapel*
> *January 7, 2007*

137. *I, but no longer I*

I think that what happens in Baptism can be more easily explained for us if we consider the final part of the short spiritual autobiography that St. Paul gave us in his *Letter to the Galatians*. Its concluding words contain the heart of this biography: *"It is no longer I who live, but Christ who lives in me"* (Gal 2:20). I live, but I am no longer I. . . . this phrase is an expression of what happened at Baptism. My "I" is taken away from me and is incorporated into a new and greater subject. This means that my "I" is back again, but now transformed, broken up, opened through incorporation into the other, in whom it acquires its new breadth of existence.

Homily at the Easter Vigil
April 15, 2006

138. *A new identity*

Paul . . . describes the process of his conversion and his Baptism in these words: "it is no longer I who live, but Christ who lives in me" (Gal 2:20). Through the coming of the Risen One, Paul obtained a new identity. His closed "I" was opened. Now he lives in communion with Jesus Christ, in the great "I" of believers who have become—as he puts it—"one in Christ" (Gal 3:28).

Homily at the Easter Vigil
March 22, 2008

139. *With Christ*

In Baptism we surrender ourselves, we place our lives in his hands, and so we can say with St. Paul, "It is no longer I who live, but Christ who lives in me" [Gal 2:20]. If we offer ourselves in this way, if we accept, as it were, the death of our very selves, this means that the frontier between death and life is no longer absolute. On either side of death we are with Christ and so, from that moment forward, death is no longer a real boundary.

Homily at the Easter Vigil
April 7, 2007

140. *Brothers and sisters in Christ*

St. Paul's *Letter to Philemon* . . . is a very personal letter, which Paul wrote from prison and entrusted to the runaway slave Onesimus for his master, Philemon. Yes, Paul is sending the slave back to the master from whom he had fled, not ordering but asking: "I appeal to you for my child . . . whose father I have become in my imprisonment . . . I am sending him back to you, sending my very heart . . . perhaps this is why he was parted from you for a while, that you might have him back for ever, no longer as a slave but more than a slave, as a beloved brother . . ." (Phlm 10:16). Those who, as far as their civil status is concerned, stand in relation to one another as masters and slaves, inasmuch as they are members of the one Church have become brothers and sisters—this is how Christians addressed one another. By virtue of their Baptism they had been reborn, they had been given to drink of the same Spirit and they received the Body of the Lord together.

Encyclical letter On Christian Hope (Spe Salvi), *no. 3*
November 30, 2007

24. Reflections on the Eucharist

141. *Holy things for the holy*

In the liturgy of the ancient Church, the distribution of Holy Communion was introduced with the words *Sancta sanctis*: the holy gift is intended for those who have been made holy. In this way a response was given to the exhortation of St. Paul to the Corinthians: "A man should examine himself first; only then should he eat of the bread and drink of the cup . . ." (1 Cor 11:28).

> *Homily for the Solemnity of Corpus Christi*
> *May 26, 2005*

142. Communion

He is the one same Christ who is present in the Eucharistic Bread of every place on earth. This means that we can encounter him only together with all others. We can only receive him in unity. Is not this what the Apostle Paul said . . . ? In writing to the Corinthians he said: "*Because the loaf of bread is one, we, many though we are, are one body, for we all partake of the one loaf*" (1 Cor 10:17). The consequence is clear: we cannot communicate with the Lord if we do not communicate with one another. If we want to present ourselves to him, we must also take a step towards meeting one another.

Homily at the Italian National Eucharistic Congress
May 29, 2005

143. Manifestation

Once again, I must return to the Eucharist. "Because there is one bread, we, though many, are one body," says St. Paul (1 Cor 10:17). By this he meant: since we receive the same Lord and he gathers us together and draws us into himself, we ourselves are one. This must be evident in our lives. It must be seen in our capacity to forgive. It must be seen in our sensitivity to the needs of others. It must be seen in our willingness to share. It must be seen in our commitment to our neighbors, both those close at hand and those physically far away, whom we nevertheless consider to be close.

Homily at the Twentieth World Youth Day, Cologne
August 21, 2005

144. *The bread of Christ*

Bread made of many grains contains also an event of union: the ground grain becoming bread is a process of unification. We ourselves, many as we are, must become one bread, one body, as St. Paul says (cf. 1 Cor 10:17). In this way the sign of bread becomes both hope and fulfillment.

Homily for the Solemnity of Corpus Christi
June 15, 2006

145. *Communion*

As St. Paul says, "Because there is one bread, we who are many are one body, for we all partake of the one bread" (1 Cor 10:17). Union with Christ is also union with all those to whom he gives himself. I cannot possess Christ just for myself; I can belong to him only in union with all those who have become, or who will become, his own. Communion draws me out of myself towards him, and thus also towards unity with all Christians. We become "one body," completely joined in a single existence.

Encyclical letter God Is Love (Deus Caritas Est), *no. 14*
December 25, 2005

146. *The breaking of the bread*

It is the Apostle of the Gentiles who assures us that, with regard to the Eucharist, he is presenting not his own teaching but what he himself has received (cf. 1 Cor 11:23). The celebration of the Eucharist implies and involves the living

Tradition. The Church celebrates the eucharistic sacrifice in obedience to Christ's command, based on her experience of the Risen Lord and the outpouring of the Holy Spirit.

> *Apostolic Exhortation* The Sacrament of Charity
> (Sacramentum Caritatis), *no. 37*
> *February 22, 2007*

147. *Christian life as a living sacrifice*

St. Paul's exhortation to the Romans . . . is a concise description of how the Eucharist makes our whole life a spiritual worship pleasing to God: "I appeal to you therefore, my brothers, by the mercies of God, to present your bodies as a living sacrifice, holy and acceptable to God, which is your spiritual worship" (Rom 12:1). In these words the new worship appears as a total self-offering made in communion with the whole Church. The Apostle's insistence on the offering of our bodies emphasizes the concrete human reality of a worship which is anything but disincarnate.

> *Apostolic Exhortation* The Sacrament of Charity
> (Sacramentum Caritatis), *no. 70*
> *February 22, 2007*

148. *Eucharistic consistency*

"Do not be conformed to this world but be transformed by the renewal of your mind, that you may prove what is the will of God, what is good and acceptable and perfect" (Rom 12:2). In this way the Apostle of the Gentiles emphasizes the link between true spiritual worship and the need for a new way of understanding and living one's life. An integral part of the eucharistic form of the Christian life is a new way of thinking, "so that we may no longer be children tossed to and fro and carried about with every wind of doctrine" (Eph 4:14).

Apostolic Exhortation The Sacrament of Charity
(Sacramentum Caritatis), *no. 70*
February 22, 2007

149. *Presence*

As the Apostle Paul reminded us in his Letter to the Corinthians . . . in every Eucharist . . . we "proclaim the Lord's death until he comes" (cf. 1 Cor 11: 26). We travel on the highways of the world knowing that he is beside us, supported by the hope of being able to see him one day face to face, in the definitive encounter.

Homily for the Solemnity of Corpus Christi
June 7, 2007

25. Reconciliation

150. *The Sacrament of Reconciliation*

You will also learn, as the Apostle Paul says, to let yourselves be reconciled with God (cf. 2 Cor 5:20). Especially in the Sacrament of Reconciliation, Jesus waits for you to forgive you your sins and reconcile you with his love through the ministry of the priest. By confessing your sins humbly and truthfully, you will receive the pardon of God himself through the words of his minister. What a great opportunity the Lord has given us with this sacrament to renew ourselves from within and to progress in our Christian life! I recommend that you make good use of it all the time!

Message to young Catholics in the Netherlands
November 21, 2005

151. *Reconciliation*

The Apostle introduces himself as an ambassador of Christ and clearly shows precisely how, in virtue of Christ, the sinner—that is each one of us—is offered the possibility of authentic reconciliation. "For our sakes God made him who did not know sin" he said, "to be sin, so that in him we might become the very holiness of God" (2 Cor 5:21). Only Christ can transform every situation of sin into newness of grace.

Homily for Ash Wednesday
February 21, 2007

152. Mysterium pietatis *(Mystery of compassion)*

The duty of the priest and the confessor is primarily this: to bring every person to experience the love of Christ, encountering him on the path of their own lives as Paul met him on the road to Damascus. We know the impassioned declaration of the Apostle to the Gentiles after that meeting which changed his life: "[he] loved me and gave himself for me" (Gal 2:20). This is his personal experience on the way to Damascus: the Lord Jesus loved Paul and gave himself for him. And in Confession this is also our way, our way to Damascus, our experience: Jesus has loved me and has given himself for me.

Address to participants in a course on the
Sacrament of Penance
March 16, 2007

VII. "PRAY WITHOUT CEASING"
(1 THES 5:17)

26. Prayer in the Christian Life

153. *Prayer*

Recalling the words of St. Paul: "So neither he who plants nor he who waters is anything, but only God who gives the growth" (1 Cor 3:7), may we always glimpse through prayer the true source of commitment in charity and by it, verify its authenticity.

Address to the assembly of organizations for
aid to the Eastern churches
June 21, 2007

154. *Pray without ceasing*

[Paul says to the Thessalonians, "Pray without ceasing."]
The other recommendations would lose their power and
coherence were they not sustained by prayer. Unity with
God and with others is built first of all through a life of
prayer, in the constant search for "the will of God in Christ
Jesus for us" (cf. 1 Thes 5:18).

Homily at the Basilica of St. Paul Outside-the-Walls
January 25, 2008

155. *Liturgical prayer*

St. Paul once said we do not even know what to ask for:
"we do not know how to pray as we ought" (Rom 8:26);
we do not know how to pray or what to say to God. God,
therefore, has given us words of prayer in the Psalter, in
the important prayers of the Sacred Liturgy, and precisely
in the Eucharistic liturgy itself. Here, he teaches us how to
pray. We enter into the prayer that was formed down the
centuries under the inspiration of the Holy Spirit and we
join in Christ's conversation with the Father. Thus, the Liturgy, above all, is prayer: first listening and then a response,
in the Responsorial Psalm, in the prayer of the Church and
in the great Eucharistic Prayer.

Lenten meeting with the clergy of Rome
February 22, 2007

156. *Sacred reading and prayer*

It is important to read Sacred Scripture in a very personal way, and really, as St. Paul says, not as a human word or a document from the past as we read Homer or Virgil, but as God's Word which is ever timely and speaks to me [cf. 1 Thes 2:13]. It is important to learn to understand in a historical text, a text from the past, the living Word of God, that is, to enter into prayer and thus read Sacred Scripture as a conversation with God.

Address to seminarians at the Roman Major Seminary
February 17, 2007

157. Lectio divina

In another text of the Letter to the Philippians, at the beginning of the great hymn about the Lord, in which the Apostle tells us: "Your attitude must be that of Christ" (Phil 2:5 [Greek text: *"touto froneite"*]), you must enter into the *"fronesis,"* the *"fronein,"* the thinking of Christ. We will then be able to share together in the Church's faith, because with this faith we enter into the Lord's thoughts and sentiments, to think together with Christ.

Reflection at the Eleventh Ordinary General
Assembly of the Synod of Bishops
October 3, 2005

27. Reflections on Mary

158. *The Mother of Jesus*

[In the Letter to the Galatians], St. Paul said: "God sent forth his Son, born of woman" (Gal 4:4). Origen commented: "Note well that he did not say, 'born *by means of* a woman' but 'born *of* a woman'" (*Comment on the Letter to the Galatians*, PG 14, 1298). This acute observation of the great exegete and ecclesiastical writer is important: in fact, if the Son of God had been born only "by means of" a woman, he would not truly have taken on our humanity, something which instead he did by taking flesh "of" Mary. Mary's motherhood, therefore, is true and fully human. The fundamental truth about Jesus as a divine Person who fully assumed our human nature is condensed in the phrase: "God sent forth his Son born of woman." He is the Son of God, he is generated by God and *at the same time* he is the son of a woman, Mary. He comes from her. He is *of* God and *of* Mary. For this reason one can and must call the Mother of Jesus the Mother of God.

Homily for the Solemnity of Mary, Mother of God
December 31, 2006

159. *Our Mother*

"When the time had fully come," he wrote, "God sent forth his Son, born of woman" (Gal 4:4). The Church contemplates in the "woman" the features of Mary of Nazareth, a unique woman because she was called to carry out a mission that brought her into very close contact with Christ: indeed, it was an absolutely unique relationship, because Mary is Mother of the Savior. Just as obviously, however, we can and must affirm that she is our Mother because, by living her very special maternal relationship with the Son, she shared in his mission *for us* and *for the salvation of all people*.

Homily for the Solemnity of Mary, Mother of God
December 31, 2007

INDEX

(Numbering refers to the sequential positioning of each thought.)

RELATED TITLES

Pope Benedict XVI: Spiritual Thoughts

Spiritual Thoughts captures Pope Benedict XVI's spiritual life and his extraordinary intelligence as expressed in the first year of his papacy. His thoughts begin to unlock the mystery of his papal legacy. The short reflections from his talks, homilies, and writings are prayerful, sometimes forceful, and always satisfying. **English: No. 5-765, 128 pp.**

Mary

Spiritual Thoughts Series

Embrace Mary, the mother of God and all Christians! Pope Benedict XVI shares his thoughts on Mary as the mother of God in this book. Let the Holy Father's explanation of the special Catholic understanding of Mary's mystery enrich your faith journey. For all Christians who want to learn more about Mary. **English: No. 7-054, 180 pp. (est.)**

The Saints

Spiritual Thoughts Series

Be inspired by Pope Benedict XVI's thoughts about ancient and modern saints. The Holy Father shows how the saints glorified God despite difficulties. Find faith, cling to hope, and learn to love as you read these selections on the saints from the Pope's writings, speeches, and sermons. A book for all Christians. **English: No. 7-055, 128 pp. (est.)**

To order these resources or to obtain a catalog of other USCCB titles, visit *www.usccbpublishing.org* or call toll-free 800-235-8722. In the Washington metropolitan area or from outside the United States, call 202-722-8716. Para pedidos en español, llame al 800-235-8722 y presione 4 para hablar con un representante del servicio al cliente en español.